RECIPES FROM QUILTERS

a book of postcards

Intercourse, PA 17534
Printed in Hong Kong

Design by Dawn J. Ranck

RECIPES FROM QUILTERS: A BOOK OF POSTCARDS
Copyright © 1995 by Good Books, Intercourse, Pennsylvania 17534
International Standard Book Number: 1-56148-166-1

INTRODUCTION

Amid the rush and haste of life, many people seek rest and quiet in community life. Quilters find community in common goals and activities. They talk of needles and thread, fabric and stitches, and bedcovers and pieces of art. They gather in homes, fabric shops, and convention centers to share their ideas and projects.

Many quilters are also homemakers. Some treat both cooking and quilting as high art forms. Others work hard to prepare varied and healthful meals for their busy families and quilt when they have free time.

Those who love to quilt and those who love to cook will share in the special vibrancy of this small collection.

—Louise Stoltzfus

SPINACH-STUFFED SHELLS

Makes 10 servings

12-oz. pkg. jumbo shells
2 10-oz. pkgs. frozen, chopped spinach
15-oz. carton ricotta cheese
8 ozs. mozzarella cheese, shredded
1 tsp. salt
1/4 tsp. pepper
1/2 lb. ground beef or turkey
32-oz. jar spaghetti sauce

1. Cook shells according to package directions. Drain.
2. Prepare spinach according to package directions. Cool slightly. Stir in ricotta cheese, mozzarella cheese, salt and pepper.
3. When shells are cool enough to handle, stuff each one with 1 Tbsp. spinach-cheese mixture. Arrange in shallow baking pan.
4. In skillet over medium heat cook ground beef or turkey until browned. Drain any excess fat. Stir in spaghetti sauce and heat through. Pour meat sauce over stuffed shells.
5. Bake at 350° for 30 minutes or until bubbly.

© 1995 Good Books, P.O. Box 419, Intercourse, PA 17534 • 800/762-7171

Artwork by Cheryl Benner.
Recipes from *Favorite Recipes from Quilters* by Louise Stoltzfus.
To order Cookbook use information on divider line.

HOMEMADE WHITE BREAD

Makes 2 large loaves

1 1/2 Tbsp. yeast
1 tsp. sugar
2 cups lukewarm water
1/3 cup cooking oil
1/3 cup white sugar
1 Tbsp. salt
5-6 cups flour

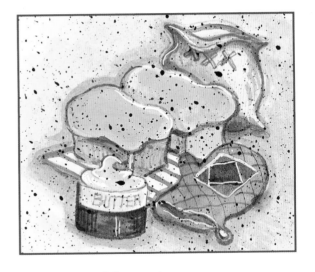

1. Sprinkle yeast and sugar into 1 cup lukewarm water. Let stand for 10 minutes.
2. Pour yeast mixture into large bowl and add all ingredients, kneading well. If dough is too sticky, add a little more flour. Place in greased bowl and cover with cloth.
3. Let rise 1 hour or until doubled in size. Punch down. Let rise again until doubled in size.
4. Form dough into 2 loaves and place into large greased loaf pans. Let rise again until nicely rounded in pans.
5. Bake at 350° on lower oven rack for 25 minutes. Remove from oven and butter tops lightly. Immediately remove bread from pans.

© 1995 Good Books, P.O. Box 419, Intercourse, PA 17534 • 800/762-7171

Artwork by Cheryl Benner.
Recipes from *Favorite Recipes from Quilters* by Louise Stoltzfus.
To order Cookbook use information on divider line.

CHEESY TURKEY CHOWDER

Makes 6 servings

2 turkey wings or 1 turkey drumstick
1 tsp. salt
1 medium onion, chopped
1 cup chopped carrots
1 cup chopped celery
1 cup chopped potatoes
4 Tbsp. butter
6 Tbsp. flour
2 cups milk
1 cup shredded cheddar cheese

1. In a large saucepan cook turkey, salt and onion in water to cover. Simmer until meat is tender.
2. Remove meat from broth. Cool, debone and dice into small pieces. Set aside.
3. If needed, add water to broth to make 4 cups. Add carrots, celery and potatoes and simmer until tender.
4. Melt butter. Stir in flour. Gradually stir in milk until well blended. Add to turkey broth, along with the cheese, and cook over medium heat until thickened, stirring constantly.
5. Add turkey meat to chowder and heat through. Serve.

© 1995 Good Books, P.O. Box 419, Intercourse, PA 17534 • 800/762-7171

Artwork by Cheryl Benner.
Recipes from *Favorite Recipes from Quilters* by Louise Stoltzfus.
To order Cookbook use information on divider line.

Shoofly Pie

Makes 1 9" pie

1 cup flour
$^2/_3$ cup brown sugar
1 Tbsp. shortening
1 egg
$^3/_4$ cup molasses
$^3/_4$ cup boiling water
1 tsp. baking soda

1. Mix together flour, brown sugar and shortening until crumbly. Reserve $^1/_2$ cup crumbs. Arrange remaining crumbs across bottom of greased 9-inch pie pan.
2. In a bowl combine egg, molasses, boiling water and baking soda. Mix well and pour into pie pan. Cover with remaining crumbs.
3. Bake at 350° for 30 minutes.

© 1995 Good Books, P.O. Box 419, Intercourse, PA 17534 • 800/762-7171

Artwork by Cheryl Benner.
Recipes from *Favorite Recipes from Quilters* by Louise Stoltzfus.
To order Cookbook use information on divider line

Deep-Dish Brownies

Makes 36 small brownies

$3/4$ cup butter
$1^1/2$ cups sugar
$1^1/2$ tsp. vanilla
3 eggs
$1/2$ cup flour
$1/2$ cup cocoa
$1/2$ tsp. baking powder
$1/2$ tsp. salt
1 cup peanut butter chips

1. Cream together butter, sugar and vanilla. Add eggs and mix well. Add all dry ingredients and beat thoroughly. Fold in peanut butter chips. Spoon into lightly greased 9″ x 13″ baking pan.
2. Bake at 350° for 40-45 minutes until brownies begin to pull away from pan. Cool before cutting. Do not overbake.

© 1995 Good Books, P.O. Box 419, Intercourse, PA 17534 • 800/762-7171

Artwork by Cheryl Benner.
Recipes from *Favorite Recipes from Quilters* by Louise Stoltzfus.
To order Cookbook use information on divider line.

FRESH PEACH PIE

Makes 2 9" square pies

Crust
3 cups flour
1 cup cooking oil
1 tsp. salt
1/4 cup sugar
1/4 cup milk

Filling
2 cups water
1 cup sugar
6 Tbsp. cornstarch
4 Tbsp. light corn syrup
6-oz. pkg. peach gelatin
10-12 fresh peaches

1. To prepare crust combine all ingredients and mix well. Divide dough in half and press into 2 greased 9-inch square baking pans.
2. Bake at 400° for 10-15 minutes.
3. To prepare filling combine water, sugar, cornstarch and syrup in a saucepan. Bring to a boil and cook until thickened and clear, stirring constantly. Remove from heat and measure exactly 4 Tbsp. peach gelatin into mixture. Stir and cool slightly.
4. Core, peel and dice peaches. Fold into gelatin mixture. Divide mixture evenly between 2 baking dishes. Cool and serve.

Artwork by Cheryl Benner.
Recipes from *Favorite Recipes from Quilters* by Louise Stoltzfus.
To order Cookbook use information on divider line

GREEN CHILE CHICKEN LASAGNA

Makes 4 servings

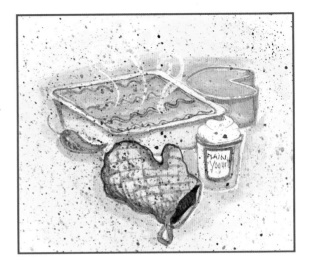

2 whole chicken breasts
6 lasagna noodles
$10^3/4$-oz. can cream of chicken soup
1 cup plain yogurt
4-oz. jar chopped green chiles
8 ozs. Monterey Jack cheese, sliced
$1/2$ cup grated Parmesan cheese

1. Boil chicken until tender. Skin, bone and shred meat into bite-sized pieces.
2. Cook noodles according to package directions. Drain.
3. Combine soup, yogurt and green chiles in small bowl. Add chicken and mix well.
4. In bottom of lightly greased 9-inch square baking dish layer $1/2$ of noodles (torn to fit pan).
   Cover with $1/2$ of chicken and yogurt mixture. Add $1/2$ of sliced Monterey Jack cheese. Repeat
   layers. Top with Parmesan cheese.
5. Bake, uncovered, at 350° for 30 minutes.

Artwork by Cheryl Benner.
Recipes from *Favorite Recipes from Quilters* by Louise Stoltzfus.
To order Cookbook use information on divider line.

Broccoli Cauliflower Salad

Makes 20 servings

Salad
8-10 slices bacon
1 head broccoli
1 head cauliflower
1 cup grated cheese
1 small onion, diced

Dressing
1/2 cup sour cream
1/2 cup mayonnaise
1/2 cup sugar

1. Fry, drain and crumble bacon.
2. Chop broccoli and cauliflower into large serving dish. Add bacon, cheese and onion and toss.
3. Thoroughly mix all dressing ingredients. Pour over salad and mix well. Serve.

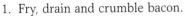

© 1995 Good Books, P.O. Box 419, Intercourse, PA 17534 • 800/762-7171

Artwork by Cheryl Benner.
Recipes from *Favorite Recipes from Quilters* by Louise Stoltzfus.
To order Cookbook use information on divider line

Caramel Pudding

Makes 2-4 servings

2 Tbsp. butter or margarine
1/2 cup brown sugar
1 cup milk
1 Tbsp. cornstarch
1 egg, beaten
1 Tbsp. cold water
1 tsp. vanilla
Pinch salt
2 bananas, sliced
1/2 cup chopped nuts

1. Cook butter and sugar together over medium heat until smooth and bubbly.
2. In a medium bowl combine milk, cornstarch and egg, beating until smooth.
3. Carefully add cold water to butter and sugar mixture. Gradually add milk mixture, stirring constantly over medium heat until mixture thickens and begins to boil.
4. Remove from heat and stir in vanilla and salt. Cool slightly and pour into serving dish.
5. Top with sliced bananas and chopped nuts and serve.

Artwork by Cheryl Benner.
Recipes from *Favorite Recipes from Quilters* by Louise Stoltzfus.
To order Cookbook use information on divider line.

CHOCOLATE PUDDING DESSERT

Makes 6-8 servings

1 cup sugar or less
2 Tbsp. cocoa
2 tsp. flour
3/4 cup hot water
1 tsp. vanilla
Pinch salt
1 cup flour
2 Tbsp. cocoa
3/4 cup sugar or less
2 tsp. baking powder
2 Tbsp. cooking oil or melted margarine
2/3 cup milk
1/4 cup chopped nuts or chopped dates

1. In a saucepan combine 1 cup sugar, 2 Tbsp. cocoa, 2 tsp. flour and hot water. Bring to a boil and cook for 1 minute. Add vanilla and salt and cool slightly.
2. In a bowl combine 1 cup flour, 2 Tbsp. cocoa, 3/4 cup sugar, baking powder, oil and milk. Pour into greased 9-inch square baking pan. Sprinkle with nuts or dates. Pour hot syrup over batter.
3. Bake at 350° for 25-30 minutes or until baked through.
4. Serve with ice cream or whipped topping.

© 1995 Good Books, P.O. Box 419, Intercourse, PA 17534 • 800/762-7171

Artwork by Cheryl Benner.
Recipes from *Favorite Recipes from Quilters* by Louise Stoltzfus.
To order Cookbook use information on divider line

A Favorite Luncheon Turkey Salad

Makes 12 or more servings

2$\frac{1}{2}$-3 lb. turkey
20-oz. can water chestnuts
2 lbs. seedless grapes
2 cups sliced celery
2-3 cups toasted, slivered almonds
3 cups mayonnaise
1 Tbsp. curry powder
2 Tbsp. soy sauce
2 Tbsp. lemon juice (optional)
Lettuce
20-oz. can pineapple chunks, drained
Fresh mint leaves (optional)

1. Cook, cool and bone turkey. Cut into bite-sized pieces. Drain and slice water chestnuts. Remove grapes from stems.
2. Combine turkey, water chestnuts, grapes, celery and 1$\frac{1}{2}$-2 cups toasted almonds.
3. In a separate bowl mix mayonnaise, curry powder, soy sauce and lemon juice. Combine with turkey mixture. Chill for several hours or overnight.
4. Spoon onto a bed of lettuce arranged on individual serving plates. Sprinkle with remaining almonds and garnish with pineapple chunks and mint leaves.

Artwork by Cheryl Benner.
Recipes from *Favorite Recipes from Quilters* by Louise Stoltzfus.
To order Cookbook use information on divider line.

MINESTRONE

Makes 8-10 servings

2 garlic cloves, crushed
4 green onions, finely chopped
2 Tbsp. chopped fresh parsley
2 carrots, sliced
1 large onion, chopped
4 celery stalks, diced
1/4 cup olive oil
28-oz. can whole tomatoes, undrained
2 quarts water
16-oz. can refried beans
1 cup uncooked pasta
Salt and pepper to taste

1. In large saucepan sauté garlic, onions, parsley, carrots, onion and celery in olive oil.
2. Chop tomatoes. Add chopped tomatoes with juice, water and beans to saucepan with vegetables. Cook on low for 2 hours, stirring frequently.
3. Stir in pasta and cook 1 more hour, stirring occasionally. Season to taste and serve.

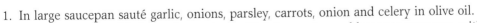

Artwork by Cheryl Benner.
Recipes from *Favorite Recipes from Quilters* by Louise Stoltzfus.
To order Cookbook use information on divider line

CARAMEL SWEET POTATOES

Makes 4-6 servings

4 medium sweet potatoes
3 Tbsp. butter
2 Tbsp. cornstarch
1 cup firmly packed brown sugar
1 cup water
1/4 tsp. salt
1/2 tsp. nutmeg

1. Cook and peel potatoes and cut lengthwise. Place in greased, shallow baking dish.
2. Combine all remaining ingredients in a saucepan and cook slowly until thickened, stirring constantly. Pour sauce over potatoes.
3. Bake at 350° for 25-30 minutes, basting as needed.

© 1995 Good Books, P.O. Box 419, Intercourse, PA 17534 • 800/762-7171

Artwork by Cheryl Benner.
Recipes from *Favorite Recipes from Quilters* by Louise Stoltzfus.
To order Cookbook use information on divider line.

ORANGE BREAD

Makes 2 loaves

1 cup sugar
$1/2$ cup butter
2 eggs
1 cup sour cream
Rind of 1 orange, grated
2 cups flour
1 tsp. baking soda
$1/2$ cup sugar
Juice of 1 orange

1. Cream together 1 cup sugar and butter. Add eggs, sour cream and rind of orange.
2. Sift together flour and baking soda. Mix into creamed ingredients. Spoon into 2 greased medium loaf pans.
3. Bake at 350° for 50 minutes.
4. Mix together $1/2$ cup sugar and orange juice and pour over bread while still hot. Cool 10 minutes and invert. Enjoy!

Artwork by Cheryl Benner.
Recipes from *Favorite Recipes from Quilters* by Louise Stoltzfus.
To order Cookbook use information on divider line

STUFFED ACORN SQUASH

Makes 8 servings

4 acorn squash
1 lb. ground beef
1 cup chopped onion
1 cup tomato sauce
1 tsp. honey
$1/2$ tsp. cinnamon
Dash nutmeg
$1/8$ tsp. ground pepper
$1/2$ cup water
$1/2$ cup seedless raisins
$1 1/2$ cups cooked rice

1. Cut squash in half and scoop out seeds and fiber. Place cut side down on greased cookie sheet.
2. Bake at 375° for 40 minutes.
3. Cook beef and onion in a skillet. Drain well. Stir in tomato sauce, honey, cinnamon, nutmeg, pepper, water and raisins. Simmer 5 minutes, stirring occasionally. Remove from heat and stir in cooked rice.
4. Remove squash from oven and turn right side up. Fill each squash with meat mixture.
5. Bake 20-25 minutes longer or until squash is tender. Serve.

© 1995 Good Books, P.O. Box 419, Intercourse, PA 17534 • 800/762-7171

Artwork by Cheryl Benner.
Recipes from *Favorite Recipes from Quilters* by Louise Stoltzfus.
To order Cookbook use information on divider line.

Pasta Pesto Florentine

Makes 4-6 servings

$1/2$ cup walnuts
3 cloves garlic
10-oz. pkg. frozen, chopped spinach
$1/2$ cup grated Parmesan cheese
$1/2$ cup olive oil
1 cup water
$1/2$ tsp. salt or more
1 tsp. dried basil

1. In food processor process walnuts and garlic until smooth.
2. Thaw and drain spinach. Add spinach and all remaining ingredients to walnuts and garlic and process until smooth.
3. Spoon over choice of cooked pasta. Serve hot or cold.

Artwork by Cheryl Benner.
Recipes from *Favorite Recipes from Quilters* by Louise Stoltzfus.
To order Cookbook use information on divider line.

SOFT PRETZELS

Makes 12 pretzels

1 pkg. fast-acting yeast
1½ cups warm water
¼ cup brown sugar
4-4½ cups flour
Baking soda
Kosher salt

1. In a mixing bowl combine yeast, warm water and brown sugar. Let stand for 5 minutes. Add flour and beat with a dough hook until smooth.
2. Let stand 5 minutes while you bring a deep saucepan full of water to a boil. (For every cup of water add 2 Tbsp. baking soda.)
3. Divide dough into 12 even pieces. Roll each piece into a long rope and twist into a pretzel shape.
4. Drop each pretzel into boiling water and boil for 10 seconds. Remove with a slotted spoon. Arrange pretzels on a greased baking sheet and sprinkle with kosher salt.
5. Bake at 450° about 8 minutes or until browned.

© 1995 Good Books, P.O. Box 419, Intercourse, PA 17534 • 800/762-7171

Artwork by Cheryl Benner.
Recipes from *Favorite Recipes from Quilters* by Louise Stoltzfus.
To order Cookbook use information on divider line.

RHUBARB APPLE PIE

Makes 1 deep-dish 9" pie

$3^1/2$ cups diced, tart apples
2 cups diced rhubarb
1 cup sugar
$^1/4$ tsp. salt
$^1/2$ tsp. cinnamon
3 Tbsp. minute tapioca
2 Tbsp. butter
Pastry for 2-crust pie

1. Combine apples, rhubarb, sugar, salt, cinnamon and tapioca and mix well. Turn into pastry-lined 9-inch pie pan. Dot with butter. Cover with pastry top and seal edges.
2. Bake at 425° for 10-15 minutes. Reduce oven temperature to 375° and bake another 30-40 minutes.

© 1995 Good Books, P.O. Box 419, Intercourse, PA 17534 • 800/762-7171

Artwork by Cheryl Benner.
Recipes from *Favorite Recipes from Quilters* by Louise Stoltzfus.
To order Cookbook use information on divider line.

PUMPKIN BANANA BREAD

Makes 1 loaf

$^1/_2$ cup sugar
1 large banana, mashed
$^3/_4$ cup cooking oil
1 cup mashed pumpkin
2 eggs
2 cups all-purpose flour
1 tsp. baking soda
$^1/_2$ tsp. baking powder
$^1/_2$ tsp. salt
2 tsp. vanilla

1. Mix sugar, banana, oil, pumpkin and eggs in large bowl. Stir in remaining ingredients until just mixed. Pour into greased loaf pan.
2. Bake at 325° for 60-70 minutes or until wooden pick inserted in center comes out clean.
3. Let cool 10 minutes. Remove from pan and cool completely before slicing.

Artwork by Cheryl Benner.
Recipes from *Favorite Recipes from Quilters* by Louise Stoltzfus.
To order Cookbook use information on divider line.

Cheese Broccoli Soup

Makes 4-6 servings

1 small onion, chopped
2 Tbsp. butter
3 Tbsp. flour
2 cups milk
2 chicken bouillon cubes
1 1/2 cups boiling water
2 cups shredded cheese
1/2 tsp. salt
1/2 tsp. thyme
1 Tbsp. garlic salt
Dash pepper
1 cup cooked, chopped broccoli

1. Sauté onion in butter until tender. Stir in flour and heat until bubbly. Gradually add milk and heat slowly, stirring constantly.
2. Dissolve bouillon cubes in boiling water. Add to white sauce with cheese, salt, thyme, garlic salt and pepper and heat through.
3. Stir in cooked broccoli and serve.

Artwork by Cheryl Benner.
Recipes from *Favorite Recipes from Quilters* by Louise Stoltzfus.
To order Cookbook use information on divider line

PINWHEELS

Makes 4 dozen cookies

2 cups sifted flour
4 tsp. baking powder
$1/2$ tsp. salt
$1/2$ tsp. cream of tartar
2 tsp. sugar
$1/2$ cup shortening
$2/3$ cup milk
2-3 Tbsp. butter or margarine, melted
2 Tbsp. sugar
1 tsp. cinnamon
Raisins (optional)

1. Sift together flour, baking powder, salt, cream of tartar and 2 tsp. sugar. Cut in shortening until mixture resembles coarse crumbs. Add milk and stir until dough follows fork around bowl.
2. Turn out onto lightly floured surface. Knead gently for $1/2$ minute. Roll out dough to $1/4$-inch thickness.
3. Spread with melted butter. Sprinkle with 2 Tbsp. sugar, cinnamon and raisins. Roll up and seal edges. Cut into $1/2$-inch slices. Arrange, cut side down, on greased baking sheet.
4. Bake at 450° for 12-15 minutes.

© 1995 Good Books, P.O. Box 419, Intercourse, PA 17534 • 800/762-7171

Artwork by Cheryl Benner.
Recipes from *Favorite Recipes from Quilters* by Louise Stoltzfus.
To order Cookbook use information on divider line.

OVEN BEEF BURGUNDY

Makes 4-6 servings

3 lbs. beef chuck roast, cut into cubes
$10^{3}/_{4}$-oz. can cream of mushroom soup
1 scant soup can dry red wine
8-oz. jar whole mushrooms, undrained
1-2 onions, cut into chunks
Salt and pepper to taste
$^{1}/_{4}$ cup cold water
$^{1}/_{4}$ cup flour

1. Place all ingredients except water and flour in 3-quart casserole dish.
2. Cover and bake at 350° for 3 hours. Stir once or twice during baking time.
3. Combine water and flour to make flour paste. If paste is not smooth, add more water. During last 5 minutes of baking time, stir flour paste into mixture to thicken.
4. Serve over hot noodles.

Variations: Substitute 8-oz. can tomato sauce and 1 pkg. dry onion soup mix for mushroom soup. Use $^{1}/_{2}$ cup red wine if desired.

© 1995 Good Books, P.O. Box 419, Intercourse, PA 17534 • 800/762-7171

Artwork by Cheryl Benner.
Recipes from *Favorite Recipes from Quilters* by Louise Stoltzfus.
To order Cookbook use information on divider line

SEAFOOD PASTA SALAD

Makes 10 servings

16-oz. pkg. pasta
1 lb. fresh shrimp
$1/2$ lb. crab meat
1 cup frozen peas
3 green onions, chopped
3 medium tomatoes, chopped
$3/4$ cup olive oil
$1/4$ cup chopped fresh parsley
$1/3$ cup wine vinegar
1 tsp. dried oregano
$1^1/2$ tsp. dried basil
$1/2$ tsp. garlic salt
$1/2$ tsp. coarsely ground pepper

1. Cook pasta according to package directions, omitting salt. Drain and rinse with cold water.
2. Steam and peel shrimp.
3. Combine all ingredients and toss gently. Chill and serve.

© 1995 Good Books, P.O. Box 419, Intercourse, PA 17534 • 800/762-7171

Artwork by Cheryl Benner.
Recipes from *Favorite Recipes from Quilters* by Louise Stoltzfus.
To order Cookbook use information on divider line.

CREAMY VEGETABLE SOUP

Makes 4-6 servings

1 Tbsp. margarine
3 medium carrots, thinly sliced
1 medium pepper, chopped
1 medium onion, chopped
16-oz. can whole tomatoes, chopped
3-4 potatoes
2 cups water
1 tsp. chicken bouillon
$1^1/_2$ cups skim milk
1 Tbsp. prepared mustard

1. In a heavy frying pan over medium heat melt margarine. Add carrots and peppers and sauté until lightly browned. Add onions and sauté until vegetables have softened.
2. Drain juice from tomatoes and add chopped tomatoes to vegetables. Continue cooking over medium heat.
3. Meanwhile, in soup kettle dissolve chicken bouillon in water. Cook potatoes in chicken broth until softened. Pour into food processor and blend until smooth.
4. Return to kettle and add milk, mustard and vegetables. Heat over low heat. Do not boil. Serve when heated through.

© 1995 Good Books, P.O. Box 419, Intercourse, PA 17534 • 800/762-7171

Artwork by Cheryl Benner.
Recipes from *Favorite Recipes from Quilters* by Louise Stoltzfus.
To order Cookbook use information on divider line

Rhubarb Pastry

Makes 8-10 servings

Crust
8 Tbsp. butter, softened
1 Tbsp. sugar
1 egg yolk
1 cup flour
$1/4$ tsp. salt
$1/2$ tsp. vanilla

Filling
2 cups fresh, diced rhubarb
2 Tbsp. butter, melted
4 Tbsp. flour
$1^1/2$ cups sugar
2 eggs, beaten
1 cup heavy cream

1. Mix together all crust ingredients and pat into 9-inch square baking pan.
2. Spread diced rhubarb over crust.
3. Combine all remaining filling ingredients and pour over rhubarb.
4. Bake at 350° for 1 hour or until set.

Artwork by Cheryl Benner.
Recipes from *Favorite Recipes from Quilters* by Louise Stoltzfus.
To order Cookbook use information on divider line

Greek Peasant Salad

Makes 6-8 servings

Salad
1 large head romaine lettuce
2 medium tomatoes, cut in wedges
1 large cucumber, sliced
6-8 radishes, thinly sliced
4-6 green onions, sliced
6 ozs. feta cheese, coarsely crumbled
1/4 lb. Greek black olives
1 tsp. minced fresh mint (optional)

Dressing
3 Tbsp. lemon juice
2 Tbsp. red wine vinegar
1 clove garlic, crushed
1/2 tsp. minced fresh oregano

1. Wash, drain and chill lettuce. Tear into large bowl. Add vegetables, cheese and olives. Sprinkle with mint.
2. Blend all dressing ingredients in small bowl with whisk. Pour over salad and toss lightly. Serve immediately.

Artwork by Cheryl Benner.
Recipes from *Favorite Recipes from Quilters* by Louise Stoltzfus.
To order Cookbook use information on divider line

HEARTY FRENCH MARKET BEAN SOUP

Makes 10-12 servings

1 lb. assorted beans
2 quarts water
1 quart chicken stock
1 Tbsp. salt
1 ham hock
2 bay leaves
$1/2$ tsp. dried thyme
28-oz. can tomatoes, chopped
2 cups chopped onion
2 cups chopped celery
1 clove garlic, mashed
8 ozs. smoked sausage, sliced
8 ozs. chicken breast, diced

1. Wash and soak beans at least 2 hours, preferably overnight.
2. In a large soup kettle combine beans, water, stock, salt, ham hock, bay leaves and thyme. Cover and simmer for $2^{1}/_{2}$-3 hours.
3. Add tomatoes, onion and celery. Cover and simmer $1^{1}/_{2}$ hours.
4. Add garlic, sausage and chicken. Cover and simmer 40 minutes. Serve.

Artwork by Cheryl Benner.
Recipes from *Favorite Recipes from Quilters* by Louise Stoltzfus.
To order Cookbook use information on divider line.

OATMEAL RAISIN BREAD

Makes 2 loaves

$1/2$ cup warm water
2 pkgs. yeast
$1^{3}/4$ cups warm milk
$1/4$ cup brown sugar, firmly packed
1 Tbsp. salt or less
3 Tbsp. margarine
5-6 cups flour
1 cup rolled oats
1 cup raisins

1. Measure warm water into large warmed bowl. Sprinkle yeast on top and stir until dissolved. Add warm milk, sugar, salt and margarine. Add 2 cups flour and beat with electric beater until smooth, about 1 minute.
2. Add 1 cup flour and oats. Beat vigorously with spoon until smooth, about 150 strokes. Add enough flour to make a soft dough. Turn out onto lightly floured board and knead until smooth and elastic, about 8-10 minutes. Cover with plastic wrap and a cloth. Let rest 20 minutes.
3. Divide dough in half and roll each into an 8" x 12" rectangle. Sprinkle $1/2$ cup raisins over each rectangle. Shape into loaves by rolling up and tucking ends under. Place into greased loaf pans and cover loosely with plastic wrap. Let rise in warm place until doubled in size, about 1 hour.
4. Bake at 400° for 30-40 minutes or until done.

Artwork by Cheryl Benner.
Recipes from *Favorite Recipes from Quilters* by Louise Stoltzfus.
To order Cookbook use information on divider line.

WALNUT GLORY CAKE

Makes 16-20 servings

$3/4$ cup flour
1 tsp. salt
2 tsp. cinnamon
9 eggs, separated
$1^1/2$ cups sugar
2 tsp. vanilla
2 cups finely chopped walnuts

1. Sift flour with salt and cinnamon. Set aside.
2. In a large mixing bowl beat egg whites until soft peaks form. Gradually add $3/4$ cup sugar and continue beating until very stiff.
3. In separate bowl combine egg yolks, $3/4$ cup sugar and vanilla. Beat until thick. Stir in dry ingredients. Gently fold this batter into egg whites. Fold in walnuts and spoon into 10-inch tube pan.
4. Bake at 350° for 55-60 minutes. This cake resembles angel food cake.

Artwork by Cheryl Benner.
Recipes from *Favorite Recipes from Quilters* by Louise Stoltzfus.
To order Cookbook use information on divider line.

VELVET CHEESECAKE

Makes 10-12 servings

1 lb. ricotta cheese
2 8-oz. pkgs. cream cheese
1 lb. sour cream
1 1/2 cups sugar
4 eggs
1 Tbsp. vanilla
3 Tbsp. cornstarch
3 Tbsp. flour
8 Tbsp. butter, melted

1. Cream together ricotta cheese, cream cheese, sour cream and sugar. Add eggs, one at a time. Add vanilla and mix well.
2. While mixer is still running, sprinkle cornstarch and flour around inside of mixing bowl. Mix in melted butter. (Batter should be thin.) Pour into greased 9-inch springform pan.
3. Bake at 325° for 1 hour. Turn off oven and let cheesecake sit for 2 hours. Remove from oven and chill before taking out of pan.

Artwork by Cheryl Benner.
Recipes from *Favorite Recipes from Quilters* by Louise Stoltzfus.
To order Cookbook use information on divider line.